Suicide: Why are you Stalking me?

Don't Fall In The Trap Of Suicide, fulfill Your Purpose

DEBORAH LA CHAPELLE-MITCHELL

Copyright © 2021 Deborah La Chapelle-Mitchell

All rights reserved. No part of this book may be reproduced, stored, or transmitted by any means—whether auditory, graphic, mechanical, or electronic—without written permission of both publisher and author, except in the case of brief excerpts used

in critical articles and reviews. Unauthorized reproduction of any part of this work is illegal and is punishable by law.

To contact the publisher please visit our website. www.trinityhillspublishing.com

Table of Contents

Introduction vi
Chapter One: From The Beginning 1
   A child's innocence 1
   Suicide: My first encounter with him 2
   He whispered to me 4

Chapter Two: Is Something Wrong With Me? 6
   Am I different? 6
   I can't do anything right 7
   I am broken/broken-hearted 9
   His second whisper 10

Chapter Three: No One Loves Me 11
   Adversity stalks me 11
   Words are thrown at me 12
   Rejection feeds me 13
   He (Suicide) gently touches my heart 15

Chapter Four: My Life Is Useless 16
   He speaks to me 16
   Why am I here? 17
   Indifference 18
   He now walks beside me 20

Chapter Five: Sudden Fear 21

Anxiety holds me tight 21
I can't do anything right 22
He (Suicide) is all I think about 24
My emotions consume me 25
He (suicide) faces me 27

Chapter Six: I am Alone In This World 28

No one loves me 28
Attacks seem personal 29
No one understands 31

Chapter Seven: I Wish I Was Never Born 33

I hate you God 33
I am better off dead 34
Self-pity holds my hand 35
I can see him (Suicide) now 36

Chapter Eight: He Brings Me To The Point Of No Return 38

He prepares me for oneness 38
I'm intimate with him (I drank from his wine) 39
It is finished, I am his 40

Chapter Nine: There's Hope In Waiting 43

The scent of water 43
Job 14:7-9 King James Version (Bible) 44
Words of Affirmation 45

INTRODUCTION
Don't fall in the trap of suicide, fulfill your purpose

This book is for the depressed, suicidal, and all who feel the need to read it either for themselves or to help someone else. It came out of my own battle with suicide as a child growing up until my late teenage years and also because of the number of young people I have worked with during Vacation Bible School who expressed similar issues. My inspiration also came from persons I have spoken to in the past who either had suicidal thoughts themselves or attempted suicide at least once in their teenage or adult life.

I am not an expert in this field or topic, neither will I pretend to be. I am just writing from my experiences and walk with Suicide to assist someone who might be suffering from suicidal thoughts like I was. I am also going to share how to track the beginning of suicidal thoughts and trail its ending before it is too late.

Throughout the chapters of my book, you will find that I talk a lot about my life as a child through my teenage years. This is because I want you to see how the spirit of suicide comes through a series of pain and trauma. It breaks you down and also breaks your will to live by diminishing your self-worth in your own eyes through the efforts of others.

As a Christian, I tend to look at the spirit behind things, and I believe that suicide is a spirit that has an agenda to pursue, overtake and devour the weak and vulnerable through a series of abusive attacks and a loss of things very dear to them.

I want to draw your attention to this; as long as we live in this imperfect world, we will have adversities. But, there is hope in waiting because nothing remains the same forever. It will get better if you hold on.

I also want you to note that you were not born to pick up space as you may have been told by someone dear to you, but that you are a designer's original and made for a perfect destiny.

I have passed by many cemeteries, and looked at the tombstones, and imagined how many of the occupants are there because of suicide.

I have passed by many cemeteries and looked at the tombstones and imagined how many of them are there because they ended their lives mainly because of what someone else did or said to them, thereby forfeiting their gifts, talents, visions, dreams, and aspirations, because they allowed themselves to become someone's dumping ground for their garbage.

I thank God every day that I did not succeed in ending my life. I was bullied at school and at home, I was abused sexually and verbally, I was used abused and rejected, was even called ugly by my then step-dad, ran away from home, and was abused again by men, but God kept me.

I finally decided to end it by drinking poison twice, I drank once, ended up in the ER, caught before I could take it the second time. What I did not know was that I was being set up to abort my purpose.

So come with me as I take you through the steps of my rundevu with Suicide and my getting set free from it to be here today to share it with you through my book entitled "Suicide, why is he Stalking me?" which I never thought I could write and never would have written if I had the chance to end it all, my pages would have been as some in the grave, EMPTY.

CHAPTER ONE

From The Beginning
A child's innocence

As a child for so many of us, our rejection may have started in the womb. Some parents, because of certain circumstances, would have tried to abort us. For some, our biological fathers ran at the first mention of our existence, or we were just spoken of as a mistake causing frustration to our parents. Whatever the situation, we were rejected by the first person whose arms we fell into.

On the day of our birth, we are now in an unfamiliar place, knowing really nothing. However, the first seed of rejection had already been unknowingly planted within us, just waiting to germinate.

For some of us, our physical, mental, sexual, and or verbal abuse began at a tender age by persons most trusted by us or trusted by our loved ones. For some, a loss of a father or mother through death leaving us with a single parent, other family members, or we just became wards of the state.

Whatever the adverse circumstance, we find ourselves feeling rejected and alone to fend for ourselves. We feel wounded, angry, hurt, bitter, and unwanted.

Those feelings pent up and without intervention robs us of our innocence and leads us into a path of destruction and mayhem. We also become vulnerable to the elements out there that have been set up for our destruction. We also can become those elements of destruction against others as well as against ourselves if we don't recognize our worth, which cannot be priced.

My seed of rejection started from the womb, my father was not around, and my mother felt trapped so, she tried to abort me, but God had a plan of which no one was aware. I had a step-father who hated me, he thought I was ugly, and, so he abused me in whatever way he felt at the time, it seemed to him that I was worthless, and I never told anyone.

Have you ever wondered why is it that when one person abuses you or calls you nasty and ugly names, after that, everywhere you go, whether school, work, friends, or foe, it's like everyone is just chomping and following suit? Well, that's the plot of the pursuant. His first method is to foster self-hate and a feeling of worthlessness within you, to make you an enemy of yourself and a lover of him. His name is 'SUICIDE' DON'T LET HIM IN!

Suicide: My first encounter with him

As a teenager, I mostly kept to myself; I became very withdrawn. Neighbors around would call me shy because of my quietness. My sister and I would often fight, but I would always let her beat me up because I was afraid of what my step-father would do if I beat her (I was always bigger than she was), she was my step-father's favorite girl.

I managed to remain by myself for long periods because I had two imaginary friends by the names of Rosley (the boy) and Sherry (the girl). My mind was so distorted that every time I played with my imaginary friends, they would almost always be abusing and torturing me. It felt very therapeutic for me.

My step father was abusive towards my mother, and as children, we would go into the bedroom, climb the walls and watch in fear and horror. I remember my heart beating so loudly in fear I could pass out; my life felt dark.

There were much more abuse and terror I encountered I will not put in this book, maybe when I write my autobiography one day should the Lord permit.

At my house, we were religious. We had to keep the Sabbath as well as all the holy Jewish days. We also had to fast for Atonement, as well as learn the ten commandments by heart and other scriptures, if we didn't, we would be punished or beaten. My sister would always rebel to my father's face but I would learn it, and he would always ask her first if she had learned it. When she said she did not learn anything my father would automatically punish both of us without asking me. However, one day I saw him strip my sister outside the house and beat her with a cord, I was so frightened that I ran from home down the Stoney hill straight to the police station.

The police came but they didn't do anything, they even saw the cord which a neighbor kept and showed them. They spoke to them and left, and as soon as they were gone I got a good licking. I felt as if I was not supposed to be there, I felt as if I did not belong there; like I should not exist. That's where I encountered the spirit of suicide he was in my thoughts for the first time, and it felt like that was the answer, that was my introduction to him.

If you will, try to remember the first time suicide crossed your mind, the very first time. Where were you? What were you doing? What was your trigger? Write it down and follow me on his trail.

He whispered to me

I would often find myself alone, mostly my choice so I could talk and play with the imaginary friends I've made, they had become my closest friends, they taunted and tortured me, but it still somehow felt better than my real life because they paid attention to me or so I thought.

During this time, I wanted to be with them all the time. My stepfather worked on mornings up until about 9 a.m., then he would come home on evenings go and hang out with his friends, and when he gets home later, he would look for us. If we were outside playing, he would call us inside, and if we were sleeping, he would wake us saying that we were 'sleeping down the house,' he made life unbearable.

One time, I was sitting on the floor by myself, he came in with my sister (his favorite) and he put his arms around her and whispered to her while looking at me, he said "she ugly eh," and he laughed, I felt broken inside, I felt as if I could just disappear, I felt like nothing, my tears filled my glasses.

Then I heard his whisper, "I am the only way out of this, you will have no more pain, I will give you my peace."

In the midst of rejection, Suicide stalks you, he always comes at your weakest moments. If people only know how much they are aiding him by mistreating others.

I rehearsed and regurgitated the whisper I heard in my ear over and over again, looking for the opportunity to take up the offer. Somehow I felt at peace when I imagined myself just not being around. In that place, nothing and no one matters, not even those dearest to you.

My adversities may not be the same as yours, for you your problems may come with a different face, the methods which may be used to bring me to entertain suicide may not be the same problems that will bring you to entertain him, we are all different and assess things differently but no matter what the cause, you must be vigilant and fight for your life and your purposeful future, it is not just you thinking about it. What bought you to hear his whisper, what happened to clear your ear to hear what you thought were your own thoughts? Did you continue to think about it as it crossed your mind?

CHAPTER TWO

Is Something wrong with me?
Am I different?

Have you ever felt different from everyone else, as if you don't belong, you don't fit in? It seems like everywhere you go someone is picking on you, all you hear is you are ugly, fat, useless, good for nothing, and so on. Have you ever seen someone who is so beautiful or handsome (if it's a guy) but when you give them that compliment they either get angry or they blatantly deny it? Well, I can tell you, I have on numerous occasions, complimented persons, especially young, beautiful women on their beauty and they became agitated, some even told me that they are not, it is so alarming.

I was once there; I had grown to hate myself. This did not happen overnight, it came as a result of years of rejection and abuse, situations and people had broken me down rendering me defenseless and open to the spirit of suicide. We are marked for death, and for many of us it will be by our own hands, and we are led to believe that no one will miss us, we are doing the world a favor.

We are made to feel as if the world is against us, we are inferior. Children and young people are bullied at school, and their self-esteem has taken an onslaught of attacks which all leads up to self-hate, feeling as if you are the ugliest, the dumbest, the most stupid like you have no hope and the biggest lie of all, you have no purpose.

Don't fall for it!!! You are no different from anyone else, it doesn't matter who you are, what you have or where you come from, it doesn't even matter what you look like, just don't surrender to suicide, you are better than that, you are not what they say you are. You are beautifully and wonderfully made by God, you have a future and a hope, but only if you wait and work at your goals and dreams.

You are not too old or too young, too fat, too ugly or not the right color, you are perfect for what you were created, so don't be afraid to explore, try new things, dream big and see those dreams come to pass. You will meet hurdles along the way, don't fret. As a great athlete, practice jumping over those hurdles, and the ones you can't jump over, use as stepping stones, and you will fulfill your dreams. But you must have dreams.

I can't do anything right

When we put too much emphasis on perfection, there is no room for shortcomings and mistakes, they are deemed as YOU ARE A FAILURE all because of what was embedded in you as a child. Some children are punished for mistakes, you may have broken a plate or glass and told that you are clumsy or stupid or you sat an exam and didn't get the results your parents were looking for, and you hear that you are dunce, stupid, good for nothing and such like. So, you grew up thinking that you are a failure.

For some, you may have been told that once you studied or worked hard, you will be anything you want to be. So you studied and studied, got your degrees only to be faced with disappointment in the job market. You feel unfulfilled, you feel like a failure. I want you to know that life is a bed of roses, there are sweet times but there will always be thorns and that is what makes it beautiful, the challenge to defy the odds that said you are stagnant and you will die there, you're a failure.

Maybe your father left your mother or your mother died in childbirth and you are the one being blamed for it. Maybe, for some reason, you blame yourself for him or her leaving, questioning if you had been a good child or would things have been different if you were not born.

You may have a disability, or you're not good at academics but your parents want you to become a doctor or a lawyer and you are frustrated so you become depressed and suicidal. Maybe even the stress of coming first in a test where you've tried your best and you repeatedly failed at it has made you depressed.

I want you to know that everyone is different, once you do your best. There is no one in this world that is born to do nothing, you can excel in your gift or field, we all have a gift.

If you try to do what you were not born to do, you will not only be miserable but, you will also not do it right. If you are thinking that you should be doing it right, then you will probably not do it right while thinking that you can't do anything right, and you will also most likely be frustrating those working with you.

'Bat in your crease', find out what you are good at and do it with all your might. Everyone has the power to get wealth, you just need to use your gifts, talents, and time to accomplish your purpose. If it's not as an employee that enjoys his/her job, then open a business, but don't stop trying. If I did, I would be dead at my own hands, because suicide is always lurking, looking for a victim; someone to believe in his lies, someone to love him more than life.

I am broken/broken-hearted

Brokenness of a person is Being Overwhelmed by grief or disappointment.

Similar meanings are defeated, beaten, vanquished, overpowered, overwhelmed, subdued, demoralized, dispirited, discouraged, dejected, crushed, humbled, dishonored, ruined, crippled.

Suicide capitalizes on certain types of emotions to have his way with us, brokenness being one of them. A broken heart, broken promises or broken dreams leaves us vulnerable to his seduction.

He is skilled in what he does and what he uses to entrap us. He is always there waiting, lurking in the darkest times of our lives so that when the time is right, we will give in to his beckoning call.

A jealous or jilted lover, who's feeling dejected and rejected fraternizes with him. A child or young person who loses his or her friends, parents, grandparents, etc. A husband or wife whose spouse has just died, leaving them with an empty broken heart. A child that just got disciplined by their parents and they feel angry and hurt. A child or young person being bullied at school or molested by someone and afraid to tell, even if they do, no one seems to be listening or helping.

Whatever our issues are, suicide is most present lurking, waiting, and whispering to you. Don't entertain him, please, because he will bring you to a point of no return. We all battle with brokenness and I know it hits us as individuals differently. I am not in your shoe and I can't say how you feel, but if you hold on and pray a lot, also, find someone you trust, and just talk things out, bit by bit the pieces will be put back together. No man is an island, we all need someone even if your brokenness tells you differently.

His second whisper

I was about fifteen years old at the time when he again whispered to me. I was so unhappy at home that I ran away and found different places to sleep for a couple of days. However, it was not for long, I had to suck it up and return home. I was so afraid but I still returned and hid in the house from my parents. Then the softness of his voice came again, "you don't have to face them you can end your life now." I immediately saw my mother's medication, and I seemed to had lost all my thoughts, all I knew was that I had to die and I could hear his whispers, "just do it now."

I opened the pack and threw out all the pills in my hands, and as I was about to put it in my mouth my sister came into the room shouted at me then she called out to my mom who was close by who took them away from me.

I felt so terrified and miserable, I felt like a failure; I couldn't even accomplish this simple task to end my life. That is how suicide operates when you don't want to confront people or problems especially when you may have done something wrong and you have to face the consequences, suicide will be most present, taunting you, wooing you, showing you his good side, he will never tell you of the real outcome and the aftermath of such a choice.

Well I am here to give a bit of a bird's eye view of what happens after suicide, after all, I am still alive, Thank God!!!

CHAPTER THREE

No One Loves Me
Adversity stalks me

Have you ever thought to yourself, "Wait, one thing after the other?" Everything seem to go wrong and without warning or time to heal, something else happens again that has you in wonder. In the Bible a man named Job encountered the same dilemma, he lost his servants, his live stocks, his children and his health in one day, what a loss huh? Losing your children and health is the worst adversity one can ever encounter?

Guess who suddenly showed up, yep, suicide. 'Why was I born?' 'curse is the day my mother brought me forth in this world,' 'I should have died at birth' were some of the thoughts and words coming out of Job's lips.

The last and greatest of suicide's attempt on Jobs life came from his wife. After losing all your possessions, children and health, the one person who was left, hopefully to be a source of strength said to him, "Why don't you curse God and die."

WOW!!! What a statement? All that would have been left for Job to do is to embrace suicide totally. After all, that's where suicide lurks, in your darkest hour, he causes adversity to be magnified in your mind and it's all in an effort to entrap you. I have felt him from time to time.

He is always right there waiting to catch you when you fall, his agenda, that you never recover from adversity, that you wallow in depression, he makes sure that he gets you before you have time to think and change your mind, which gives you a chance to succeed.

Job cancelled his appointment with suicide, he told his wife that she spoke as a foolish woman and he waited on God, giving himself time to heal, and most of all, giving God a chance to change his situation. In the end, Job regained more than he had lost, and even his friends who blamed him in his darkest hour, had to turn to him so that he can pray for them for their harsh words. When you are going through your adversities, friends and family may turn on you but don't give in to suicide, if you hold on, you will win, and those who spoke against you, will come to you for help.

Words are thrown at me

What are words? In my view, words are communicative sounds using the tongue, coming out from one person's heart to another, they can be grouped together to make sentences or statement or it can be one sound. However, long or short, words sets things into motion, either for destruction, or to build. The unique thing about words is, that once they are released, they can never be returned to the sender, by your words wheels are set into motion.

Humans, whether knowingly or unknowingly have the power to either receive what is spoken or reject it and by rejecting it I mean not letting it get into your heart. We have the power to hear but out rightly reject words. If you ask a lot of successful people they will tell you when people say they can't, they defied that and did, they were called stupid, ugly, fat, skinny etc., but that became a stepping stone for them to succeed.

Words will forever be sent out for good or bad, and I bet many bad words would be thrown at us. There are a lot of angry people in this world, there are also people on agendas; to bully you, to bring you down to the lowest. either because of jealously, or they themselves were the victims of harsh lying words or the issues of life has left them angry, willowing in self-pity or lacking self-control and they just decided to release their angry words without a care. There is a saying, 'hurting people, hurt people.

You have to work hard at not being people's garbage dump for their bad and unproductive words. Sometimes people may have received these evil and unproductive words, carrying them around like heavy burdens just looking for relief. So, they look for someone like themselves who is willing to receive them, it makes their burden lighter each time they release and you receive.

Don't be a receiver for lies, be a receiver for truth, if you receive lies you will reject truth. So, if someone says to you that you are smart, you will not believe because for a long time a person or persons said to you that you are stupid. Don't fall for that lie, 'you are what you believe.' Believe God and believe in yourself, believe you can do anything you put your mind to. If you don't you will wallow in self-pity and self-hate and suicide will just be around the corner waiting to pounce on you.

Rejection feeds me

Have you ever felt rejected? I am sure you have, it's the worst feeling in the world. Rejection makes you feel useless, ugly, hurt, empty, unworthy, lonely and you can add many more of your feelings to this list. Rejection is an awful experience and it is felt by everyone at one time or the other, however, it is experienced by each individual differently and at different levels, for many, it starts in the womb.

As a child growing up, I've always felt that I was different, this feeling was compounded by things said and done to me by my step-father, peers and other adult relatives, then, like a disease it seemed to have spread to persons on the outside. I remember one time seeing on a store front a sign saying vacancy I went in to find out what I needed to apply for the job and one of the persons looked at me and said that the vacancy had been filled, I asked her, "then why is the sign still up", she said they forgot to take it down and they were going to take it down now, I did not believe her but I said ok and left.

The next day I deliberately passed by the store to see if the sign came down, guess what? It was still up, I felt so rejected because I always had a problem with my color, I am very dark skinned and was always plump added to a low self-esteem, so of course I told myself that was the reason I was rejected, I hated who I was the more.

Feeling rejected when you don't love yourself can be one of the worst feeling you can have, it adds to your sadness and pushes you further away from everyone into a cold, dark and lonely place where you can be fed lies from suicide's whispering to you that your life is no use, you being here was a mistake, and no one loves or cares about you, and that you will not be missed if you quietly make your exit out of this world.

Don't eat of his fruit, it is poisonous, and like the apple given to sleeping beauty by the witch pretending to be an innocent old lady, one bite would put you in his sleep hold, and if no one is there to give you that true love kiss that will cause you to see your worth, you will die and forfeit your purpose. All will be written of you is the day you were born and the day you left the earth, an empty line left in the middle.

He (Suicide) gently touches my heart

As we go through life's difficult situations and circumstances, some of us feel hurt beyond repair, we feel as if we can't take life anymore, we tend to look for something to hold on to, for some it's a boyfriend, a friend, drugs, alcohol or anything that we think can keep us afloat.

Life for you is like a drowning man grasping for anything that can keep him afloat, he will snatch for a straw to keep him above water but it will not work. You see, at that point his rational thinking is off he just wants someone, something to help him live, until he gets tired and then he sinks. Water may have by now gotten into his system, and he becomes so exhausted that he gives in to death, he continues to sink as the water over takes his lungs and in seconds he is gone.

Life can be like that for many, you take and take while searching for a reason to live but then you seem to find none, so you give up mentally and emotionally, while suicide is there watching, and waiting. When he sees your mental breakdown, he gives you a soft touch as if to say, "I am here for you, just stretch forth your hand, I will reach you."

At that point your heart feels like it has made a final decision, the right one, and the touch you felt in your heart makes you feel assured that all will be well, you just have to leave this world, you need to die, you will not be missed.

Suicide is a master at what he does, he is skilled, he watches you, waits patiently for you; he is not usually pushy, he does not come in like a flood in the initial stages, he seems gentle and understanding and he seems to have all the answers for pain that no one else has. Suicide is tricky, so his touches are gentle like a cool breeze on a hot day, but he is deadly and he doesn't tell you what's on the other side, neither does he show you the pain and havoc you would leave behind.

CHAPTER FOUR

My life is useless
He speaks to me

When you are downtrodden you can hear all the negative voices over and over in your head. It's like someone is touching a replay bottom over and over in your head and you can't seem to stop it. That's his cue to step in, he now has an avenue to talk to someone who will listen, someone who will heed to his voice.

Suicide never gives up nor gives in, he is always there stalking you, waiting on the right moment to pounce on his unsuspecting victims, he puts on a comforting voice that gives you a false sense of assurance and when you entertain him and become comfortable with him he strikes you with his deadly thoughts.

Suicide is a master at his game, he knows how and when to make his move so you don't catch on easily, he cannot afford for you to have a change of heart so he moves quickly and with precision to gain you as his next victim.

Life's issues can depress you beyond your wildest dreams, some ADVERSITIES are very pressing and torturing and can cause you to look at life as a great big disappointment. It plunges you into a bout of depression and you just want out. Mr. Suicide, like a vulture, swoops down to feast on what is left of your sanity and he speaks and speaks and speaks, and at that point you just want to give up.

Life can really make you feel useless, like you were born for misery. To you, you can't do anything right, it causes you to blurt out words like, "I should have never been born", "I hate myself, I am a nobody, nobody loves or wants me." These feelings arise from a feeling of uselessness but just remember that it's just a feeling, you were created with purpose even if you don't feel like it.

Don't give up, please don't, and don't entertain Suicide, or he will take you to the point of no return.

Why am I here?

Why am I here? This is a question that everyone will ask at one point or the other in their lifetime and it is an important and natural question to ask. However, when it is asked from a broken or angered and depressed heart, the answer just doesn't come in your favor.

Pain is a universal event, when it is coming no one knows, and it doesn't ask your permission to come at you, it just shows up. Sometimes when it comes it can cause havoc in your life, some of which seems irreparable, and it leaves you in the loneliest and dark place. You feel like you are the only person in the world going through this mess. This is the place where Suicide is most present, waiting, he is subtle like a serpent just waiting; to strike, and to take you out. Suicide however, will not come harsh, he is soft, seemingly polite and patient, it's like he has all the time in the world, just for you and he will be sure to answer your question as to why you are here.

I need you to note: that Suicide spirit is not your creator; neither is he the one that gave you purpose or vision. However, he still has his own purpose and vision for your life, he will take you to a place of no return, he has the sting of death for the unsuspecting, 'Don't Surrender to Suicide.'

He will tell you that you are a mistake to this world, he says he has a new world for you where you will find rest, he will tell you that no one will miss you, you will be doing everyone a favor, he is a liar, he likes to take what is not his, but he needs your help to bring you to an end, don't let him. Ask God for strength and keep going, seek help, seek answers for your existence from the one who created you in the first place, you don't have to know him as yet, once you are sincere to know your purpose he will show you. You can make it!

Indifference

I never knew the meaning of indifference even as an adult, somehow the word never crossed my eyes, all who knows me well, knows that I am a dreamer, I never sleep without dreaming. One morning in the wee hours I dreamt that I was reading a book which looked like the Bible and two words were underlined in red, then I heard a loud voice saying there is a difference between Apathy and Indifference.

I got out of my sleep picked up a dictionary and looked it up and found Apathy to mean lack of interest, enthusiasm or concern. Simply put, a behavior that shows no interest or energy from someone and shows that someone is unwilling to take action, especially over something important. I have also found the meaning of the word indifference to mean lack of interest in something or someone concern or sympathy. They are both the same.

Though these are very similar in meaning I believe that indifference carries a bit more weight. When you are indifferent you become like an alien in your surroundings. It's like nothing moves you, like you have been tranquilized so you are unable to feel anything at all, your emotions are asleep and you just want to be away from everyone and everything. I have been there and it was around that time in my life I had that dream.

Finding the meaning of what I was feeling and putting a name to it really helped me because if you don't know what you are going through and you can't find a word for it, you will be kept longer therein as you fall deeper and deeper into the sea of indifference, and you just don't care anymore.

This is a conduit for suicide, he feeds off of your indifference, because in that state you are looking for a way out, an escape route from everyone and everything, he is just there at the right time, with his offer to take you away from all your problems, but it must be a secret, he will tell you to keep him a secret. That's why if you ask the friends and family members of those who committed suicide a lot of them will tell you that they never suspected a thing, they are left in shock wondering what went wrong, or what did they do wrong, some friends and family members never recover from the guilt they feel because they think that they should have done some things differently. I even know of some who took their lives because they couldn't live with the loss and the shame. Take some time to find out if you are in that stage of Indifference or even Apathy, and please don't keep suicide a secret, expose him to a family, friend or find someone you trust, don't let him tell you that you cannot trust anyone, that's one of his favorite lines. You can even write everything you feel, everything you are going through even the good things, you never know it can become a best seller, or you might just leave help for someone going through the same things. Whatever you do shout your feelings until you find help, but don't die in that wilderness of loneliness and abort your purpose. Shalom

He now walks beside me

Like a constant companion, suicide walks besides his unsuspecting victim, he follows you step by step, he wants to be there when you are at the edge and feeling all alone, he pretends to be that friend that sticks closer than a brother. He pledges his allegiance to you and whispers, mimicking the words of Jesus, "I will never leave you, nor forsake you, I will be with you till the end," like a song he sings softly, sweetly to you in your darkest hour.

His footsteps match yours, like soldiers marching in sync to the beat of music, so he walks with you following your every move, he is patient, seductive, subtitle and crafty in his dealings with you but the pain you feel skews your rational thinking, so you allow him to walk beside you without question.

I remember my own walk with suicide, everywhere I went it seemed like he was always with me, I reasoned with him like a close friend, he seemed to be my only companion, I hated being with anyone else, I took advantage of every chance I got to be alone with him.

That was one of the coldest and darkest seasons in my life, I never knew that a better season for me was around the corner and I thank God every day that I did not succeed in consummating my marriage with suicide, if I did, I would not have been able to write this book to help someone as wonderful and purposeful as you. Please take my hand through the pages of this book and let us walk together through the open door of destiny that's just waiting for you, for us and the many more like us. SHALOM!

CHAPTER FIVE

Sudden Fear
Anxiety holds me tight

Anxiety, my first encounter with anxiety. I was married at that time and I found out that my husband was unfaithful to me with one of his co-workers, when he finally told me about it I was devastated. The mistake I made at that time was to ask him what she had that I didn't, I was not prepared for the answer, he said that she was nice and attractive so that made me feel the opposite, that answer played over and over in my mind like a tape recorder, I couldn't shake it.

After that, I don't know what happened to me, I became afraid for no reason, I could hear my heart beating so loudly. Sometimes, without warning, I would wake out of my sleep feeling like I am having a heart attack, sweating profusely and very afraid.

This would happen to me a lot when I am alone, it made me so afraid and I kept it to myself. Now anxiety had now become a part of my existence, when it came on I felt its tight grip on me like it didn't want to let me go.

My husband was a beautiful person, the pain he brought to me he regretted but the damage was already done.

My life was changed for what seemed like forever, to date I still feel it holding on to me, but because I understand life a little better the grip feels less tight. I can now look anxiety in its face and tell him that I will no longer be yielding to his embrace until he releases me, and he does, but he returns at different intervals.

To help me with this I always use a verse in the Bible which says, "The wicked flee though no one pursues, but the righteous are as bold as a lion (Proverbs 28:1 NIV), and I say to myself Deborah, you are not wicked, no one is pursuing you so stand bold as a lion.

I can't do anything right

Life's mistakes along with strong criticism from people who do not direct you in the right path nor do they have a proper solution for your problems, or persons who seem to be there just to make your life miserable, gives you a feeling of worthlessness, you feel like you just can't do anything right.

Maybe things fall out of your hands a lot, or everything you start to do you have not been able to finish, or maybe everything just seems to go wrong in your life, just out of control, your relationships seem to not be working out, and you blame yourself because everyone else seems to be blaming you anyway, and somehow it seems as if once you are around or you are a part of something it just goes sour.

I have been there and done that and it led me closer and closer to suicide, I felt as if I could do nothing right. I was a high school dropout, every boyfriend relationship I had would just last a short while; they would all leave. I felt ugly and worthless. I was also what people would call clumsy;

throwing down things, I was seemingly dunce in school and was also bullied by my peers, just for how I looked.

No matter how hard I tried it seemed like I was just not like everyone else and I just couldn't do anything right, I became very frustrated with life, everyone else seemed to be doing well except me and it seemed like those around me were always saying mean things to me. They called me cruel names and would constantly tell me how ugly I was, I just wanted death, life was not for me.

Today, I still throw things down, one guy stayed with me and became my husband, he became my best friend, the love of my life. To him I was beautiful, I was his rib but guess what? We were married for 16 years and we were very close, then he got ill for two years, the love of my life died and left me alone, the one person who thought I was beautiful was taken away from me.

I was devastated, I was alone again or so it seemed, in my pain. That is what I saw, loneliness has come upon me again, I yearned for death, I felt that inside, but my relationship with Christ is what kept me together. So, I did not want suicide but I did still want to die.

Today, as I'm writing this book, it's been seven years since my husband died. I am not remarried neither am I in any relationship as yet, I guess I am still finding myself. I have four beautiful children God gave me; two boys and two girls along with three awesome grandchildren.

Bottom line, I did not die, not at the Lord's hands, because he has a plan and purpose for me, and certainly not at my own hands, suicide did not overtake me and I am glad. Now I am writing this book to help someone who might get this book in their hands. Suicide is always stalking you and he uses different adversities in order to get you to befriend him until he takes you to the point of no return. You must purpose in your heart to live, it will not be easy, it's an uphill battle but if you persevere you will win the prize and live out your purpose.

Seek help, I know it seems as if no one cares about you or loves you, but that's a lie, you are loved. When I wanted to die I forgot about my children who were dependent on me, suicide causes you to forget about the things that are important, but I truly believe no matter how long it takes, if you hold on, you will see the purpose to which you live. You will be happy like I am, that you lived. You will begin to see those who love you rather than who doesn't. SHALOM.

He (Suicide) is all I think about

After being bombarded by so many faces of adversities I became so fed up, I felt like I had reached my wits end. As a result, all my thoughts were directed towards suicide, it seemed like the only way out, the only way of escape, a safe place to hide, and he was always right there waiting, whispering to me.

I began to hunger and thirst for him, I thought of him: how I was going to consummate my relationship with him, what it would be like, what was the quickest and easiest way to be with him, to finally be one with him.

I would always find a way to be alone just so that I could think about him, it felt so good, I felt at ease with my thoughts, I even fell asleep thinking about suicide. When I thought about him I didn't feel like crying, my problems were no longer important, nothing and no one was on my mind anymore. The more I thought about him, the happier and at peace I felt, this had to be the right decision I was making, or so I thought.

That is how suicide operates, he comes as a solution to all your troubles, but, he never is. He never tells you the truth; what is on the other side or how much pain, turmoil and mayhem that you leave behind. He will never show you the ones who love and depend on you to always be around, he'll never show how many lives are destroyed or who will follow what you did because they believed that they will never be able to live without you.

The torcher your family, friends, siblings, spouses and others go through as a result of your decision, the shame of being looked down on, the blame some people will put upon them or even they will put upon themselves, a weight too heavy for some of them to bare, the destruction of families, divorce, separation, trauma and or duplication of what you did.

What you may be unaware of is, suicide will not stop with you, when he finishes with you he quickly moves on to his next victim and he will continue to search for other victims within your family as well as other families, he has a hidden agenda which is to destroy families, to break the family unit leaving them vulnerable and open to any other attacks which will all point persons back to him, he is a master seducer, don't let him in, be wise and be aware. Shalom.

My emotions consume me

Emotions, what is it?

Emotion is a strong feeling deriving from one's circumstances, mood or relationships with others.

If it's taken from the position of the Bible, the Greek word is Pathos meaning suffering, experience.

According to the brain, emotions such as fear and love, are carried out by the Limbic system, which is located in the temporal lobe. While the Limbic system is made up of multiple parts of the brain, the center of the emotional processing is the amygdala, which receives input from other brain functions, like memory and attention.

Your emotion is that feeling you get, when, after or during an event or experience, causing a reaction, manifested as sadness, anger, loneliness, happiness etc.

Because of all the bad experiences I've had in the past from childhood up until well into my adult life, and the fact that I never learned how to cope or how to control what I was feeling, I suffered all the more until I could not control my emotions and it was like a runaway train.

After a while, my own emotions controlled me, I cried for no reason, when people insulted me I would just laugh to cover the pain. I felt anxious and my heart would just start beating out of control, I became afraid for no reason; I felt terror. I allowed myself to be taken advantaged of because I was afraid to speak up for myself.

I would make rash decisions without thinking through, I gave of myself because I was afraid to say no, I was afraid to hurt people's feelings so I would settle for mine to be hurt instead. I would take the hurt, without question. It all caused me to choose death over life, after all, I was already dead inside and no one knew, and to me no one cared.

I was totally led by my emotions that I was void of understanding I only saw my problems, so much so, that the right side of my brain which helps me to rationalize things seemed dormant, suicide.

He (suicide) faces me

After years of walking with Suicide, I felt much closer to him now. He had just become the first person I saw each morning, evening and night and I now had a face to face relationship with him. Suicide had become my best friend in all the world, he now speaks to me face to face as a man speaks to his friend.

Our relationship had now reached another level, a higher level, we were now on the brink of becoming one or so I thought. This love affair I had with suicide was becoming more and more serious, I could feel his breath in my face, I longed for his kiss, for his sweet embrace. I thought once we became one, I would finally be happy, I didn't care about anyone else all I wanted was him. I did not tell anyone about him, if I did leave a hint it was in codes that they could not truly understand or mistake for a joke or something else.

I was happier than ever, people just thought that I had a boyfriend or I had just changed because something good happened to me; to change my mood, whatever their reasoning for my sudden change in disposition, they were happy because I seemed happy and I was happy because I was in love. It feels so good when the one you love feels the same about you and I believed he (suicide) loved me because he never left my side.

CHAPTER SIX
I am alone in this world
No one loves me

Once your focus is on suicide he becomes your only friend, he's the only one you feel loved by. My family members and friends became either my enemies or aliens; in my mind no one loved me or cared for me. To me the whole world was against me and was out to get me.

Where I was mentally, my foes were those from my own household, and any kind words said to me were just lies and mamaguy. In my mind they wanted something from me. I was a wreck and did not know it, I thought that I was in the best frame of mind and I was about to go to a better place, a place of rest.

My life was not worth anything in this world, I felt cold and alone, I was rejected, abandoned and unloved by everyone else except the love of my life, SUICIDE. He had become my safe haven, the thought of him kept me warm, I felt like I could be myself around him, I could talk to him for hours and not feel judged, he wasn't bossy or rough, he would always be right there when I needed someone, and he would always listen to my problems and he understood my needs.

Suicide would always assure me of his allegiance to me, he told me that I had a friend in him and I believed his every word, when I felt trapped by my abuser he comforted me by letting me know that I can come to him at any time to a place where abuse can't reach me and my abuser will never find me, that thought was so comforting it made me feel kind of invincible.

No one could reach me not even pain, sometimes I begged him to take me now but his response was always, "Soon, when the time is right my love, you will know for sure, then you can come." Those words made me want him even more and more. Suicide had become my freedom.

Attacks seem personal

Things have a way of happening that makes it seem as if the whole world is against us, something may be said by someone and instantly we believe that it is directed towards us. Maybe, we have done something wrong and haven't forgiven ourselves, so, as a result, everywhere we turn it seems as if people are talking about us, because we believe that everyone knows what we have done. You now look at yourself as a fugitive running from the law; the mob that is chasing you.

Suicide has a way of being right there in the midst of every situation waiting for you to turn his way. These days with the increase of technology, more people have the chance of seeing things, knowing things about people that was not so much available to their knowledge as now, social media has gained control, everyone has a phone and like a loaded gun we use it, things are uploaded about people, some true but some just plain unproven gossip.

Today you can be a very private person and tomorrow you can be the center of everyone's attention and we all know about the trolls on social media who are just there to capitalize on other people's misery, or the latest gossip (true or not). But I have learnt that in life there are all kinds of people and what they do just shows a side of them that is not good.

I still, however, cannot downplay the effects that these attacks will have on you, what I can say is look for someone to talk to, you may even have to lay low for a while just to strengthen yourself, just don't try to deal with it alone. Amidst the negativity there are some loving person/s out there who will be ready to walk you through this season to get you back on track, just don't die there. Suicide is a cold and lonely lover. Once he gets you in a good grip, at that point you most likely will not escape though you may try (have a change of heart).

Most times these attacks are not personal, it is just about the ten days' gossip that moves around, there are always persons, who, like a child with a loaded gun has a phone or computer and some juicy information (gossip) in front of them, and without waiting for the facts begin to type their opinion and perceived notions about the situation, not caring about the outcome or who it may hurt or tarnish.

Life is worth living, YOUR LIFE IS WORTH LIVING! It's important, also, nothing last forever, everything in life has a season, ask the many people who have been tortured on social media and weathered that storm, their business has become old news, now it's time for the next juicy gossip. Don't give them the opportunity to make your death and loved ones whom you have left behind the new gossip. Don't allow your children to be bullied in school by your act of suicide, they may be bullied for something you did that has made social media and their friends have seen it and you will not be there to talk or help them through the shame. If you leave, you leave them to cope on their own and they most likely will follow in your deadly path just to escape the results of your life choices.

Whatever mistakes you make in life know that there is always someone who loves you or will love you in spite of what you may have done.

No one understands

I remember talking to a young person who was going through a series of adversities throughout her lifetime, every time she talks to you about it she would always say "No one understands what I am going through." Another young person explained to me that at the time she is going through her problems she feels like she is the only person in the world, no one else is there, no one else understands; she just felt all alone. Honestly, it really feels as if no one understands your feelings.

A lot of people just listen with the intention of giving an advice or solution which the person going through their pain cannot yet assess, or understand at the time. Advisors use statements like; God has a plan, there are other people who are worse off than you, you are not the first, you need to have faith, words, let me tell you we have become accustomed to hearing. Or the classic, they begin to talk about all the things they went through, some persons adding the statement, "we didn't behave like that." There are a lot more said to people who are going through depression or mental pain; they can either rescue them or send them deeper down the path of Suicide.

We need to understand that the person who is going through their stress is going through 'THEIR STRESS'. Everyone asses' things differently, and at the time of your problems, you can't see anything or anyone else, it's like you are in a bubble that no one can reach, you are just floating around meaninglessly, helplessly, aimlessly and in your mind you want to talk about it but you feel like no one either cares, it's to shameful, painful or they just would not understand.

To the person who is experiencing this, don't listen to that voice in your head that's saying: no one will understand. Someone will understand and help you, don't resort to listening to those suicidal voices in your head. Most times you have the answers you are looking for. Ask yourselves questions and then write down the answers, write how you feel, draw, paint, or even play music. For those who believe in God, talk to him, for those who don't, ask him if he is real give you a real encounter with him so he can help you. What I'm saying is; do something, anything to keep your head above water, until you feel comfortable to talk to someone.

To those who are chosen to be the listeners, please just listen, ask questions that will help the person to think and answer for themselves. They have the solutions, it's just that they can't think clearly at that time; they are hurting. Let them vent if they want to and don't pretend to have all the answers, don't use your life as a yard stick for theirs, just be there as much as you can when they need to talk, after all, they chose you. If it's too much for you then please ask them first if you can get someone else involved, maybe a professional, and most of all, don't disclose their personal secrets; be trustworthy.

CHAPTER SEVEN

I wish I was never born
I hate you God

I can't tell you how many times I have told God that I hated him because in my mind I couldn't understand how my life could be so miserable and there is a God. I had concluded, it's either there is no God or he hates me like everyone else hates me. But deep down in my heart I believed he was real so I believed the latter; he just does not love me. After all, I've had experiences with fathers, in that my own father was not around, and the one I thought God gave me as a step- father, treated me with such contempt.

God seemed so far from me, so, I decided to live my life without him, all the men I knew were evil, even God, I did not know the love of a father and in my opinion that is the love that is needed for a child to even begin to understand his/her worth. Fathers are looked upon like superman in the eyes of a child. And looks have nothing to do with it, to his child he is super.

The man I called daddy was to me like Freddie Krueger, he tortured me in so many different ways, even in my sleep. Due to how he treated me I believed that God was the same, if he loved me, he would kill my stepfather.

Years later, I got to know God for myself and he saved my life, I could have been dead. I would never have been able to write this book to help someone else who may be going through the same experience, I now know the love of a Father. Life is full of pain because we live in a fallen and imperfect world, so we will get all the imperfections which comes along with it.

Suicide is an enemy that we don't want to play with, and all the Adversities like depression, abuse, loss etc., are just ways used to lead someone to Suicide. Don't be a statistic.

I am better off dead

I couldn't see the purpose for my life, everything seemed like a chore, even taking a bath. The only thing that felt comfortable at that time was sleep, even though I would go to bed tired and wakeup just as tired, nothing interested me, not my friends nor family members, (in fact, I did not have much friends anyway). I felt as if I was covered by a black, thick, wet blanket, and I was in a deep black hole, all at the same time.

People would just tell me how ugly I was and how fat I was. You know there are people who just like to give their opinion where it's not needed or requested; saying the wrong thing and at the wrong time. Well, I got a lot of those kinds of unsolicited opinions, nothing was going right for me. I was not working and I was pregnant (in the very early stages) my life was a literal mess.

In my mind it would be best if I was not around, I did not believe that anyone would miss me if I left. I hated myself, how I looked, I hated my voice, I was too fat, too short, and way too black, God made me the worst out of everyone else. Those were my thoughts, my conclusion; this world will be a better place without me, I will be better off dead, for my sake and everyone else's sake also.

These are the thoughts that would bombard my mind daily but it was all a lie, a set up to lower me into the trap of suicide, I thank God every day for my life. The struggles and trials continue to beat down on me but because I know that I am not alone in this journey, because God is with me and has given me his peace, I can continue to live, love and be loved. I am not who I was back then, I have grown, and I am surely not what the enemy says I am. I know who I am and whose I am and that makes me strong. You are stronger than you think, get to know Jesus he will help you to find yourself, receive his joy, for in it lies your strength.

Self-pity holds my hand

There was a time when I felt so sorry for myself, I couldn't understand why this was happening to me, and I felt as if I was the only person this was happening to and no one understood my pain. In the state of pitying myself I could not and would not see anyone else's pain, I just couldn't help anyone else, why should I? After all, no one was helping me.

Wallowing in self-pity caused me to see my friends and family as enemies because I felt as if they were supposed to be there for me all the time, at this point I should be the center of their attention, but it looked as if they were ignoring me, their life is perfect and mine is in a mess, yet they seem to be about their own business.

I got so comfortable in that state, I thought I couldn't come out, I felt stuck. Every day I complained and complained, nothing was enough for me. I had nothing to thank God for not even my life because I just wanted nothing to do with living. I just wanted to die, and even trying death seemed like a failure because I was still alive.

No one felt sorry for me so I felt sorry for no one, I was too busy with myself and my own feelings. Well, self- pity was another road which led me to continue my love affair with suicide, I believed that one day soon our relationship would be consummated, and I would be one with him. He encouraged me to continue with self-pity, he said I had all rights to feel sorry for myself, he understood my pain and he was with me all the way.

He whispered to me, "Soon my love, soon we will be together, where no one can reach you, and no one can hurt you anymore." I felt very comfortable with self-pity, it had become part of me, and it helped me to shut out everyone and everything around me, I just saw me and my problems.

I can see him (Suicide) now

After building such a close relationship with so many of Suicide's family members: (fear, self-pity, loneliness etc.,) over the years, I was now allowed to see him in a physical sense. I now knew what he looked like, he allowed his family members to prepare me to meet with him face to face, I could now put a face to the love of my life and he was to die for.

He was very appealing and mighty fine to look at, he was everything I dreamed him to be and then some, his expressions were so tender, his smile warm yet firm. He was strong, he was a take charge kind of guy, he was also very authoritative, his smile made me blush. He expressed his love to me over and over and over again, he told me that he needed me, he needed my love, he said that he couldn't live without me, his words made me feel so special, like I was his one and only.

We talked for hours without any interruptions, we spoke about how I was feeling. He understood me like no one else did, he never told me that I was wrong for feeling how I felt, he said I had all rights. He even showed me things I didn't even see, like how people looked at me, he would always tell me that no one loves me, only him, he even told me how I should feel about what was done to me.

All I did was stare at him, he had so much charisma which also made him easy to love. I just wanted him to stay forever. I longed to be with him and him alone always and forever and I rested in the thought that I would soon be with him forever, the countdown was on.

It hurt me to know that I had to leave his presence to go about my daily routine, but each day I would pray for that day when I could stay with him, when all is done. In the meantime, I kept to myself as much as I could because he told me that he got jealous when I spoke to anyone else too much. Suicide wanted to be my best friend, my only friend and the love of my life.

CHAPTER EIGHT

He brings me to the point of no return
He prepares me for oneness

After my last meeting with Suicide he was all I could think of during that day, I became extremely happy throughout that day. I was so overwhelmed with happiness that it was visible to all who I came in contact with, some people laughed with me while others questioned my sudden boost of happiness, because prior to this I was reserved, with a sad demeanor most of the time.

I began to give stuff away that was dear to me, it didn't matter because where I was going I wouldn't need them anymore but they didn't understand, and I couldn't tell them our secret. I remembered Suicide telling me that I cannot tell anyone because they would be jealous of us and take me away from him, and they would continue to torcher me, he said that he knew for a fact that they did not love or care for me, only he does and I believed him with all my heart, I loved and trusted him.

No one could find out and I did all I could to keep them in the dark, in my mind I said, they hurt me, they payed me no mind, part of me felt that they would miss me but I didn't care, even if that was true, I planned to make them suffer for ignoring me and doing me wrong.

At that point, anger, hurt, resentment and self-pity held on to me. They were my companions sent to comfort me by my love; suicide, and they said that they were sent to prepare me. The time had come for me to be with my love, to become one with him. They hurried me so I had to leave what I was doing and go to the place designated to meet with him, to finally be one with him, so I ran, I couldn't wait. I didn't even say goodbye, I couldn't, they wouldn't let me for fear I may give the secret away, or change my mind.

I'm intimate with him (I drank from his wine)

This day started like any other. I got up, I had breakfast and left home, I visited a friend and spent some time with him, we laughed and talked as other times, nothing was different (to him it was), but for me I was just saying my goodbyes without actually saying it to him. at times I felt distant from him and he felt it too, he did ask a couple of times if I was okay but the answer was always the same, "Couldn't be better."

After a few hours we said our goodbyes and I asked him for a hug, he obliged. This hug was longer than usual, we smiled at each other and I left for home. I spoke to a few persons on the way, very briefly though because I was in a hurry, the time was at hand. I felt the presence of my love, his call was distinct, no more time wasted, my love was waiting and I couldn't wait any longer to be with him, I knew that he was preparing a place for me where we can be intimate, where no one can see or interrupt us.

As I reached my front door I could feel his presence even more stronger, he was waiting for me. As I got inside I passed my mom and my stepfather, as soon as I saw him I felt this anger inside. But It was quickly pushed away by the peace I felt with the thought of meeting with my soulmate. So, I gave my greeting and headed away to the place prepared for me but before I could disappear, my step-father started to lay out chores for me to do as soon as I changed my clothes and the manner in which he said it, aggravated me even more. If I had any second thoughts about where I was about to go, they just jumped out the window, the final door was closed. I said okay to him nicely and left.

As I reached my room, suicide was there waiting for me as promised, he called to me with his fingers, he whispered to me to be quiet and to move quickly, I dropped my bag and followed him to the bathroom, and locked the door behind me. There was a glass prepared for me to drink it looked like red wine, I took it from his hands and drank it, it tasted bitter but he encouraged me to drink all of it, he said, to drink quickly before my step-father came looking for me. So I drank it all, he then kissed me, so tenderly and I began to feel this sweet sleep overtaking me as his kiss became deeper and deeper.

It is finished, I am his

I gave into the temptation of suicide, the deadly deal was over or so I thought, so I expected, I just wanted everything to be over, that included my own life. I detested ME! MY color. I felt so dark and ugly, people told me that I was ugly, I felt so unwanted that suicide was the only and best option for me, I couldn't see pass him. After all, suicide led me to believe that I was just going back to where I came from, wherever that was, I was sure it would be better than here.

When I opened my eyes I was not where I expected to be, not at all where I wanted to be, I was still in the land of the living. I was at the hospital. I was so angry and disappointed, I even felt a little ashamed, thinking,

What's going to happen now? Will I be going back to that house? I just wanted to die, and I couldn't even accomplish that simple task.

I cried every day after that and I still looked for another chance. How could I face everyone after this, the voices in my head became even louder and louder, when is this pain I felt going to end. Not long after, I left the hospital with my mother and we went home, my step father was there, he just stared at me, he said nothing, at this point I wish he did, my mom began to quarrel with me, she was so angry, she couldn't understand what happened and why.

I did try it again a few months later, I tried to swallow some tablets my mother had gotten for her pregnancy, my hands were shaking so badly, my sister caught me and called my mother so I failed again, suicide had lost me again. Finally, I left home at the tender age of sixteen, I suffered out there but I was a lot stronger, and I now had a son to live for and a baby on the way, I was still very much alone but somewhere inside I believed it would get better although at that time I was very much going through hell.

I had hope because of my babies, and hope kept me alive, and I learned to pray more than ever, I had too, those little people depended on me and the abuse I went through at the hands of my step father, I had to make sure they didn't go through that. I didn't want suicide to attract their attention and leave me, I knew he could attract them through other adversities but I was determined to be there for them and do my best to try to protect them as best as I could, I now had one reason to live. Please look for one reason to live, in the end you will be glad you did. HOPE!

You can even have a vision for yourself, something that you would love to do or become in the future, lose yourself in working at it in order for it to come through. Write it down where you can look at it every day to encourage you to wait for it, speak to your future positively every day and always, Always, have a plan B along with an accountability partner, and most importantly, pray without ceasing. Just keep hope alive, don't let this light go dim.

CHAPTER NINE

There's hope in waiting
The scent of water

"As the hart (deer) panteth after the water brooks, so panteth my soul after thee, O God."

Psalm 42: 1 King James Version (Bible)

I first heard this topic (the scent of water) from Rev. Don Hamilton in one of his messages to our congregation, this message was about keeping hope alive through the scent of water while going through your dry and weary land. The context of this draws from the hart, this remarkable animal can smell the scent of water from miles away and as long as he has that scent he has hope of quenching his thirst, and thereby saving his life. However, sometimes when he reaches his destination for the hope of water, he is disappointed because although the water is there it is filled with mud so he can't get the water he needs.

We go through similar experiences in life. It often looks as if we are finally getting through with something positive, then without warning it becomes fruitless and we are again plunged into another disappointment. When the deer realizes that there is no water, he uses his keen sense of smell to find another source of water, and he goes after it until he is finally successful and his thirst is quenched. So must we also use our God given gifts to overcome our obstacles and reach for the stars, never quit, you are more than a conqueror, you are kings and queens in the earth.

Another thing about the hart, when hunted by hound dogs they always look for a brook or river to escape danger. On reaching the brook, they throw themselves into the water so that the dogs behind them will lose their scent. They are also known to submerge their bodies under the water, leaving only their nose above the water in order to breath in hopes that they will not be detected.

So also, we must submerge ourselves in Christ in order to escape the enemy of our souls, make him your hiding place when wounded or lost while you regroup and enter the battle again, it doesn't matter who you are or where you came from, we all go through trials and disappointments and if you don't have a hiding place you will be devoured by your foes.

Job 14:7-9 King James Version (Bible)

7. For there is hope of a tree, if it be cut down, that it will sprout again, and that the tender branch thereof will not cease.

8. Though the root thereof wax old in the earth, and the stock thereof die in the ground;

9. Yet through the scent of water it will bud, and bring forth boughs like a plant.

If you allow suicide to get a foothold in your life then hope is lost, you will never know what you would become as said in verse 10: But man dieth, and wasteth away: yea, man giveth up the ghost, and where is he?

Your life matters you only die once and you only have one life to live in this world let's make it matter. Leave a good legacy for someone to remember you by, don't give up, we all have a following, whether we know it or not and they just might follow in your footstep. If the deer and the stock that is cut down can be revived by that scent of water, you can be revived by hope, its ok to day dream big for yourself and work at making those dreams a reality.

To those who are being bullied, a lot of young people each year have committed suicide or have tried, look around, those that were successful at taking their lives because of a bully or bullies, took their dreams and aspirations with them and the bully often moves on to become what they want, they have children to carry on their generation, some have good jobs, money etc., and while you are no more, some may even move on to bullying someone else. You have the right to live, have kids and fulfill dreams like everyone else, never let anyone rob you of those experiences, no one.

Words of Affirmation

Application:

Psalm 119:11 reads

Thy word have I hidden in my heart, that I might not sin against thee

I am a designer's original, there is no one else in the world who is exactly like me

I am built to last

I am not a mistake

I was born for greatness

I was born with a purpose to which I must fulfill

When I die I must die empty {Myles Monroe}

I am not devil's food

I am destined for greatness

I am who I am because of Christ

My words are full of power

Whatever I believe and speak will come to pass

Once God is for me who can be against me

I am loved by God

I am beautifully and wonderfully made by God

No weapon that is formed against me shall prosper

God has not given me a spirit of fear but of love, power and a sound mind

I am made in the image and likeness of my heavenly Father

I have a purpose and a destiny to fulfill

I can do all things through Christ who strengthens me

I lack nothing I have everything that pertains to life and Godliness

Practical Application:

- I will speak what I want to accomplish until it comes to light

- I will write down the vision and see it come to pass

- I will speak no negative word against myself nor others

- I will replace every evil thought with thoughts of good towards myself

- I will not allow anyone to overpower me or conquer me with their evil opinions and intentions

- I will first show love to myself so that I can genuinely show love for others

- I will rise up early, spend time with God, make declarations over my life

Get dressed and fulfill purpose for my life for today and my future

- I will not waste time on things and people that doesn't add value to my life and future

- I will keep myself tidy, my hair styled and (for those who wear makeup) put some on and go out even if it is just outside my house

- I will exercise, eat as well as I can and do something that will bring me enjoyment

- With each accomplishment I make, I will build an altar there, e.g. {write it down, keep a record, or buy something and keep it in a special place as a reminder of what I have accomplished} and always celebrate no matter how small

- I won't tell anyone about my vision unless they are part of me accomplishing that vision or I know for sure they would help and support me (be very careful and ask the Lord for discernment) {some persons are vision killers whether intentionally or unintentionally}

- I will not procrastinate. In Trinidad we have a saying don't leave for tomorrow what you can do today

- I will always put my hands to work. (you may not always know what gift you will find within yourself)

- I won't ever underestimate myself and what I can do and accomplish through my gifting

(You can write books that would change a life, minister to someone on the edge and save their life etc. The point is, it doesn't matter who you are or what you look like, you are important to someone whether you know it or not, whether you've met the life you will change or not, we will all leave an impact in the life or lives of others, let it be a great one. Let the legacy you leave live beyond you, bring peace, hope and love in a world that is already lacking good mentors and role models and love. Let's not do what the mass is doing, like the blind leading the blind and they all falling into a ditch, let's be different by bringing hope to the hopeless.)

Prayer for assistance:

Heavenly Father, I humbly come into your presence today broken and in need of your assistance, I can't help myself and no one in this life can help me at this point, I need you. Father your word saids a broken and contrite heart you will not despise so here I am, your word also said that I was created in your image and likeness but right now I don't think I look like you, I prayer that you will restore me so I can look like you again.

Heavenly Father, you promised that once we come back to you, our sins, you will move as far from us as the East is from the West, Father I ask you to remove my sins far from me, wash me that I may be clean again. Father you have created me with purpose, I belong to you. Have mercy upon me that I may live and not die until my purpose is accomplished, and I have touched and impacted the lives you created me to impact.

Heavenly Father, please teach me to wait upon you so that my strength shall be renewed within me, and I will mount up with wings like the Eagle, I will run and not be weary and I will walk and not faint. And help me to remember that you are always with me, helping me so even when I walk through the valley of the shadow of death I will fear no evil. Most of all, help me to acknowledge you in all my ways that you will direct my path. Teach me self-control and help me to remain a part of the vine, Oh Father, please bring me faultless against that day of Jesus Christ and help me to know the precious love of the Father. I ask these things in the mighty name of Jesus Christ.

Amen

Prayer for acceptance:

If you have not accepted Jesus Christ as your Lord and personal Savior and you want to have a relationship with him just say this prayer with me.

Heavenly Father, I come to you today humbly confessing that I am a sinner in need of a Savior, I understand that I have walked contrary to your word and I made myself an enemy of God, Father I ask that you will hear my prayer and forgive my sins so that I may know you and become a child of your kingdom, Father I heard about the sacrifice that your son Jesus Christ made for me and I want to say thank you. Save me, heal me, wash me in his precious blood and make me whole again. I ask this in Jesus's name.

Amen

www.ingramcontent.com/pod-product-compliance
Lightning Source LLC
LaVergne TN
LVHW041555070526
838199LV00046B/1973